Winston Churchill

A Life from Beginning to the End

The Biography

History Hub

CONTENTS

Part One: Editor Foreword

We hope you enjoyed listening to this guide from Fireside Reads as much as we enjoyed bringing it to you. Our philosophy is to always delight and over-deliver, so here's one final bonus for you.

Please do us a favor and leave a review. It is critical in helping others find out about this book. We would like to help them save time as it has helped you. If you do, we will rush you these valuable bonuses: *(Worth $99 Retail)*

Attention: Get Your Free Gift Now

Every <u>purchase</u> now comes with a FREE Bonus Gift

2020 Top 5 Fireside Books of the Year

(New-York Times Bestsellers, USA Today & more)

Chapter One: Birth and Early Childhood

Did You Know?

Winston Churchill had struggles getting accepted in military school. He performed poorly in most of his academic subjects except for history and English composition; in addition to that, he had a hard time dealing with foreign languages. In a narrative about him, Churchill talked about a two-hour-long Latin test where he wrote the number of questions, he left blank beside his name and "a blot and several smudges." He flunked his entrance examination twice at the Royal Military faculty at Sandhurst. However, as they claim, the third time's a charm as he eventually qualified with the assistance of a military tutor, albeit just for the cavalry class.

†††

On the 30th of November 1874, Sir Winston Leonard Spencer Churchill, more popularly known as Winston Churchill, was born at Blenheim Palace (a home given by Queen Anne to Churchill's ancestor, the Duke of Marlborough) in Oxfordshire, England. His parents were British and American.

Winston's father was a British Lord named Randolph Churchill, the youngest son of John, the 7th Duke of Marlborough. He was elected as the Conservative Member of Parliament for Woodstock in 1873. He was a Tory radical (Tory is a person who holds a political philosophy known as Toryism, based on a British version of traditionalism and conservatism) and coined the term tory democracy. Lord Randolph died due to pneumonia. They even tried to find a cure for his sickness around the world, but they have failed. He died in Westminster shortly before Christmas.

On the other hand, Winston's mother was an American, named Jeanette "Jennie" Jerome, an independent-minded New York socialite. In contrast to the Churchills's noble bloodline, her ancestors fought for the independence of American colonies under George Washington's armies. She's the daughter of Leonard Jerome, a wealthy American businessman who's also a New York financier, avid horse-racing fan, and a partial owner of the New York Times. Lady Randolph Churchill married George Cornwallis-West and became known as Mrs. George Cornwallis-West in 1900. Having their marriage dissolved, she used her prior married name, Lady Randolph Churchill, through a deed poll (legal document binding only to a single person or several persons collaborating to express an actual intention).

Winston had a younger brother named Jack who was known as "Fighting Jack Churchill" and "Mad Jack." During World War II, he fought as a British Army officer who carried with him a longbow, bagpipes, and a Scottish broadsword.

Winston grew up in Dublin, Ireland, where his grandfather, John Spencer-Churchill, the appointed Viceroy of Ireland, employed his father as a private secretary. He stayed in Dublin from age two to six. Most of the time, the family traveled between homes, moving from Ireland to the Isle of Wight off England's southern coast to Blenheim Palace and to London. In line with the preceding, Winston's brother, Jack, was born in Dublin in 1880.

In the 1880s, Winston's parents were very active within their social circle but were emotionally distant, so the brothers were constantly left under the care of their nanny, Elizabeth Everest. She was hired by the family a month after Winston's birth and had since devoted most of her life in the family's service to the point that she never married. One of her first jobs was for the family of Thompson Phillips, whom she raised and assisted for 12 years. As Winston's parents became more neglectful of their responsibilities to their children, she stood as their second mother. The Churchill siblings were very fond of Ms. Everest and called her "Woom" or "Womany." Winston once said that"she had been [his]dearest and most intimate friend during the twenty years [he] had lived." Ms. Everest stayed with the family until 1893 when she abruptly left to go back to the Thompsons. On the 3rd of July, 1895, she died due to an inflammation of the peritoneum (abdomen's lining of the inner wall, and the cover of abdominal organs).

Winston was a sensitive child who suffered from a minor speech impediment. He started boarding at St. George's School in Ascot, Berkshire at seven years old but did poorly academically and behaviorally. Just like any other kid, he wasn't fond of going to school. After two years at St. George's, he was sent to a school in Brighton, run in a distinctive manner by two sisters, Kate and Charlotte Thomson, where he learned about things he liked, such as French, history, poetry,, where he learned about things he liked, such as French, history, poetry, horseback riding and swimming. He transferred to

Brunswick School in Hove in 1884, where his academic performance improved and then to Harrow School afterwards.

From an early age, Winston already showed an interest in military affairs and its history. His earliest surviving letter was written at the age of seven to thank his mother for the presents filled with army with their flags and castles, and toy soldiers, which he loved and collected. He had an army of around 1,500 Napoleonic-era toy soldiers, which he used to play and reenact battle scenes.

Fireside Question 1

Winston's parents were very active within their social circle but were emotionally distant, so the brothers were constantly left under the care of their nanny, Elizabeth Everest. If the brothers grew up with more attentive and affectionate parents, do you think that would somehow affect Winston's behavior towards school? Explain why.

_____

_____

_____

_____

_____

_____

_____

_____

_____

Fireside Question 2

†††

Winston Churchill was a British-American. His father was British while his mother was an American. How do you think a bi-racial environment influenced the young Winston? What American sensibilities and British qualities did he carry into adulthood?

_____

_____

_____

_____

_____

_____

_____

_____

_____

_____

Fireside Question 3

†††

Winston Churchill did very poorly in academics during his early days at school and only showed interest in the subjects he liked, such as history and English. Do you think that the theory of multiple intelligences could be applied to the young Winston? What specific intelligence did he possess? How could he be encouraged to learn the subjects he was least interested in?

Fireside Question 4

†††

Winston Churchill grew up in Dublin, where Jack was also born. They have been constantly moving between their homes in Ireland to the Isle of Wight off England's southern coast to Blenheim Palace and to London. If you were in his position, how would you feel about always being on the move? How did this affect his social development as a child?

_____

_____

_____

_____

_____

_____

_____

_____

_____

_____

Fireside Question 5

†††

Just like any other kid, Winston Churchill showed a keen interest in military affairs and its history. He collected Napoleonic-era toy soldiers and reenacted battle scenes using them. How did this interest manifest into his career choices later on in life?

_____

_____

_____

_____

_____

_____

_____

_____

_____

_____

Chapter Two: Adolescence, Teenage and Adult Years

Did You Know?

Clementine Ogilvy Spencer - Churchill stood as Winston's partner in crime and lifesaver. In 1904, she met her spouse at the age of 19 in a dance where Churchill, 29 years old, was present. Though he was already known as a member of the Parliament with great ambition and for his remarkable escape from imprisonment during the Second Boer War, Clementine wasn't impressed with him. He did not ask her to dance and just stared at her. After four years, they met once again at a dinner party where they ended up liking each other and got married in 1908. In their 57 years of marriage, she repeatedly helped her husband resolve not only his political but also his personal troubles. She stood by his side through their union, sharing her opinions and views about everything he did. Thus, Winston himself credited her as the primary driver behind his many successes.

††††

Winston Churchill was infamous for his rebelliousness and for poorly performing in his first two schools. In April 1988, he attended Harrow School, a boarding school near London, where he narrowly passed. He then joined its Harrow Rifle Corps, which set him up for a career in the military. He devoted his last three years at Harrow in military training as per his father, Lord Randolph Churchill's wishes.

Being academically challenged, entering a military school posed a great challenge for Churchill. He failed the admissions examination at the Royal Military Academy at Sandhurst twice. He was eventually accepted on his third attempt with the help of a military tutor, albeit only as a cadet in the cavalry in September 1893. He graduated from the Royal Military Academy in 1895. However, with this success came the death of his father in January 1895. He idolized Lord Churchill and mourned his father's death for quite a while despite their distant relationship.

Churchill became a second lieutenant in the 4th Queen's Own Hussars regiment of the British Army based at Aldershot at the age of 21. His eagerness for action in the field got him posted into the combat zone through the influence of his mother. In the same year, he and Major-General Sir Reginald Barnes, a cavalry officer in the British Army who served in several and commanded a number of battalion (Imperial Yeomanry, the 10th Royal Hussars, the 111th Brigade) and three divisions, were sent to North America to report on the Cuban Independence War. They became involved in a crossfire between the Cuban fighters and the Spanish soldiers. He went to New York afterward and wrote to his mother how delightful and extraordinary America and its citizens were.

In October 1896, he went to India when his regiment was stationed in Bombay for 19 months. He visited Calcutta three times and joined expeditions to Hyderabad and the Northwest Frontier. Churchill also volunteered to join Bindon Blood's Malakand Field Force in Britain's campaign against the Mohmand rebels in the Swat Valley of North-West India as a journalist. During this period, he wrote his first book, The Story of the Malakand Field Force: An Episode of Frontier War, describes a navy marketing campaign with the aid of using the British military at the North West Frontier (now Western Pakistan and Afghanistan) in 1897, which received incredible reviews. He also wrote his only work of fiction entitled, Savrola, a Ruritanian romance that chronicled the events in the capital of Laurentia, a fictional European State, as unrest against the dictatorial government of President Antonio Molara turned to a violent revolution. According to Roy Jenkins, British author and politician was a leading member of the cabinet before becoming president of the European Community and later a founding father of the Social Democratic Party, Churchill embraced writing to cope with depression, which he referred to as his "black dog."

Through his widening network in London, he was able to join General Kitchener's campaign in Sudan as a journalist for The Morning Post. Later on, he fought in the Battle of Omdurman, a demonstration of the superiority of a highly disciplined army equipped with modern rifles, machine guns, and artillery, marking Britain's success in reconquering Sudan. He also involved himself with the 21st Lancers, Britain's cavalry regiment in Cairo. He then returned to England and wrote The River War, published in 1899, about the history of the British Imperial movement in Sudan and the Mahdist War between the British Forces led by Lord Kitchener and the opposition composed of the Dervish forces led by Khalifa Abdallahi Ibn Muhammad.

With the discovery of bountiful diamond and gold mines in the Boer States, Churchill predicted the outbreak of the Second Boer War and the consequent establishment of the Boer Republics. Thus, he visited South Africa again as a journalist for The Morning Post. In 1899, he was captured and interned in Pretoria's prisoner of war camp. After two months, he managed to escape by stowing away aboard freight trains and hiding in a mine. He made it safely to Portuguese East Africa and attracted so much publicity due to this feat. In January 1900, he was appointed as a lieutenant in the South African Light Horse regiment and joined forces with Sir Redvers Henry Buller during the Siege of Ladysmith, - a protracted engagement in the Second Boer War.. Together with the Duke of Marlborough, Churchill's cousin, he demanded and received the surrender of 52 Boer prison camp guards. Wanting to be viewed with "generosity and tolerance," he publicly reprimanded anti-Boer prejudices. Upon his return to Britain, his Morning Post official report was headlined as London to Ladysmith via Pretoria.

Churchill also started reading the works of Plato, Charles Darwin, and Thomas Macaulay. His resulting interest in the British Parliamentary affairs made him ally himself with the Tory Democracy wing of the Conservative Party. He gave his first public speech for the party's Primrose League in Bath. As he started his parliamentary career, he became more active at Conservative meetings. He was chosen as one of the party's two congressional candidates for the June 1899 by-election in Oldham Lancashire. Upon being chosen as one of the Conservative candidates at Oldham in the October 1900 general election, he was appointed as a Member of Parliament by the age of 25. he stood once more. In the same month, he published a book about his South African expeditions entitled Ian Hamilton's March, which later became the focus of a lecture tour in Britain, America, and Canada.

Fireside Question 6

†††

Winston Churchill failed his entrance examinations twice when he was trying to get into the Royal Military Academy of Sandhurst. He had to employ a military tutor to get in and was only appointed in the cavalry class. Why was Churcihill so bent on getting admitted into the Royal Military Academy? What is its historical legacy?

_____

_____

_____

_____

_____

_____

_____

_____

_____

_____

Fireside Question 7

Lord Randolph Churchill died the same year his firstborn, Winston, graduated from military school. How did it affect his pursuit of a military career?

_____

_____

_____

_____

_____

_____

_____

_____

_____

_____

Fireside Question 8

†††

Winston Churchill used writing as his coping mechanism for depression. Being a journalist paved the way for his literary writing career. What led to Churchill's depression? How did writing help him cope? What other ways of coping with depression could you think of?

_____

_____

_____

_____

_____

_____

_____

_____

_____

_____

Fireside Question 9

†††

In 1899, Churchill was captured and interned in a prisoner of war camp in Pretoria. After two months, he managed to escape by stowing away aboard freight trains and hiding in a mine. Why was his escape heavily publicised? What was its significance to the British empire?

_____

_____

_____

_____

_____

_____

_____

_____

_____

_____

Fireside Question 10

†††

Upon being chosen as one of the Conservative candidates at Oldham in the October 1900 general election, he was appointed as a Member of Parliament, by the age of 25. What strengths did Churchill possess that enabled him to become a Member of Parliament at a young age?

_____

_____

_____

_____

_____

_____

_____

_____

_____

_____

Chapter Three: Career, Professional and Family Life

Churchill lived a meaningful life and died at age 90 due to a stroke on the 24th of January 1965. He had already suffered different complications as he grew old. He wasn't even healthy anymore during World War II; he had a heart attack in 1941 and pneumonia in 1943. Winston then suffered a major heart attack while still in office in 1953. Most of the national newspapers prepared his obituary but did not use it until later when he died in his London home after a severe stroke.

†††

Winston Churchill's military career started even before he went to the Royal Military Academy of Sandhurst, as he dedicated his three years in Harrow School to the Harrow Rifle Corps. In 1895, he served the armed forces as part of the Fourth Queen's Hussars regiment, was deployed to the Indian Northwest Frontier and Sudan, and fought in the Battle of Omdurman in 1898.

Writing campaign reports in the military paved the way for Churchill's literary career. He wrote a couple of reports for the Pioneer Mail and Daily Telegraph and two memoirs namely, The Story of the Malakand Field Force (1898) and The River War (1899). After the release of his second book, he left the Army and worked as a war correspondent for The Morning Post. When he reported on the Boer War in South Africa, he was held captive by the Boers during the scouting expedition but later escaped after traveling 300 miles to the Portuguese territory in Mozambique. In 1900, he published Savrola, his only novel, and then his first significant work, a biography of his father, Lord Randolph Churchill. Included in his work is the famous portrait of his great ancestor, the Duke of Marlborough, published in four volumes between 1933 and 1938. His chronicle of the First World War, The World Crisis, also appeared in four volumes between 1923 and 1929 while his memoirs from the Second World War were condensed into six books published from 1948 to 1954. After he retired from the service, Churchill wrote A History of the English-speaking Peoples in four volumes from 1956 to 1958. His orations were anthologized in dozens of volumes in The Unrelenting Struggle published in 1942, Dawn of Liberation in 1945 and Victory in 1946. He also made his autobiography entitled My Early Life in 1930 and wrote about paintings as a pastime in 1948.

Churchill became a member of the British Parliament under the Conservative Party in 1900. Following in his father's footsteps, his sense of integrity made him a supporter of various social movements. His doubt of the Conservative Party's commitment to social justice led him to join the Liberal Party in 1904, and in 1908 he got elected again as a Member of Parliament. He was subsequently elected to the Prime Minister's cabinet as President of the Board of Trade where he joined the newly appointed Chancellor, David Lloyd George, in opposing the expansion of the British Navy. Instead, they proposed the modernization of their fleets by building oil-powered warships instead of coal-powered ones. For this innovation, he was named as the First Lord of the Admiralty in 1911. Some reforms for the prison system were also started by him. He also introduced the first minimum wage rate and helped with labor exchanges and unemployment insurance set up—the People's Budget introduced taxes on the wealthy to pay for new social welfare programs. In 1915, he resigned from the government after the disastrous Battle of Gallipoli. After World War I, Churchill served as the Minister of War and Air and a Colonial Secretary under Prime Minister David Lloyd George. The factions within the Liberal Party led to his defeat as a Member of Parliament in 1922 resulting in his return to the Conservative Party. When he was ousted from the government in the 1920s, Churchill took up painting and as the years went by, he created over 500 works of art. He later wrote, "Painting came to my rescue in a most trying time."

During the 1930s, known as Churchill's" wilderness years", he focused on his writing career and published his memoir and the First Duke of Marlborough's biography. During this period, he began his celebrated A History of the English-Speaking Peoples, though it was published twenty years later.

During World War II, Churchill became the leading advocate for British rearmament. He was appointed as the First Lord of the Admiralty and a member of the War Cabinet on the 3rd of September, 1939, when Britain declared war on Germany, and by 1940 he became the Chairman of the

Military Coordinating Committee. A few months after, on the 10th of May 1940, he replaced Arthur Neville Chamberlain, a British flesh presser of the Conservative Party who served as Prime Minister of the UK from May 1937 to May 1940, upon his resignation. King George VI appointed him as Prime Minister and Minister of Defense, serving the office from 1940 to 1945. He led the country through the Second World War until Germany's surrender. Afterwards, he formed an alliance of cabinet leaders from the Labor, Liberal, and Conservative parties. He delivered one of his most iconic speeches to the House of Commons on the 18th of June 1940, warning that The Battle of Britain was on the horizon. He kept the resistance against the Nazis and formed alliances with the USA and the Soviet Union.

By March 1941, Churchill was able to secure vital U.S. aid through the Lend-Lease Act, which allowed Britain to buy military paraphernalia from the United States on credit. He created a good diplomatic relationship with the U.S. President Franklin D. Roosevelt, as he was confident that the Allies would emerge victorious. Closely working with U.S. President Roosevelt and Soviet leader Joseph, he plotted their war strategy and developed a vision of the postwar world. Despite Germany's defeat, Churchill still lost the general election in July 1945. He subsequently became the leader of the opposition party and continued to influence world affairs. He became the Prime Minister for the second time in October 1951 and served as the Defense Minister of defense until January 1952. During his postwar term, Churchill introduced reforms such as the Mines and Quarries Act of 1954 that greatly improved the working conditions in mines, and the Housing Repairs and Rent Act of 1955, which established the standards for housing. Queen Elizabeth II also knighted him in 1953. Within the same year, he received the Nobel Prize for

Literature for prolific literary work,which "defended exalted human values" and showcased his "mastery of historical and biographical descriptions".

Churchill married Clementine Ogilvy Hozier after a short courtship. They had five children together: Diana, Randolph, Sarah, Marigold, and Mary. On the 24th of January 1965, he died at the age of 90 in his London home nine days after a severe stroke episode. His health problems manifested as early as 1941 when he suffered a heart attack, and again two years later, when he had a similar attack while battling pneumonia. By the age of 78, he had a series of strokes at his office, and even though he was able to recover, he was physically and mentally wearing down. He retired as a Prime Minister in 1955. It was suspected that he had Alzheimer's disease, but most doctors reasoned that it could be just the side effect of having multiple strokes.

Fireside Question 11

Churchill mentioned that painting came to his rescue in his most trying time. What makes this activity therapeutic for most people?

_____

_____

_____

_____

_____

_____

_____

_____

_____

Fireside Question 12

†††

Churchill married Clementine Ogilvy Hozier after a short courtship. Share your thoughts about getting married after a brief courtship. Are you in favor of this or not?

_____

_____

_____

_____

_____

_____

_____

_____

_____

_____

_____

Fireside Question 13

†††

Churchill was known to have worked even in his later years and did at the age of 90. He suffered from various diseases such as heart attack, pneumonia, and multiple strokes. What do you think motivated him to work despite old age?

_____

_____

_____

_____

_____

_____

_____

_____

_____

_____

Fireside Question 14

†††

To win against Germany, he allied with the USA and the Soviet Union and closely worked with President Roosevelt and Joseph Stalin. What advantages did the Allied Powers have over the Axis Alliance. What led to the victory of the Allied Powers? .

_____

_____

_____

_____

_____

_____

_____

_____

_____

_____

Fireside Question 15

†††

Winston Churchill resigned from being the First Lord of the Admiralty after the disastrous Battle of Gallipoli in 1915 and subsequently got reappointed during World War II. Why was he reconsidered for the post? What made him the best candidate for the job?

_____

_____

_____

_____

_____

_____

_____

_____

_____

_____

Chapter Four: Main Difficulties to Overcome in Life

Did You Know?

Nobel Prize Awardee for Literature and an accomplished artist. Winston Churchill was awarded the Nobel Prize in Literature in 1953 "for his mastery of historical and biographical description as well as for brilliant oratory in defending exalted human values." He is also the only British Prime Minister to have won the Nobel Prize in Literature since its inception in 1901. He started a new passion in his 40s, painting, and eventually created 500 murals in his last 48 years. The National Trust Collections holds some of his works.

††††

Raised by aristocratic parents, Clementine Hozier Churchill's early life was lonely and marred by rumor and scandal. Her parents, Lady Blanche Hozier and Henry Montague Hozier gravely despised each other. They were known for being unfaithful, and people doubted whether Lady Hozier's children were fathered by Henry, who left his family when Clementine was just six years old. Furthermore, Lady Hozier, a notorious gambler, caused not only financial but also social problems. Due to Lady Hozier's fear that her bad reputation could harm her daughter, Clementine's wealthy aunts introduced her into high society instead.

Clementine was the driving force behind Winston Churchill's success and fame. Their story began in 1904. Clementine was 19 when she attended a dance where 29-year-old Winston was present. During this time, he was already well-known for his great ambition and for his dramatic escape from prison during the Second Boer War. Clementine wasn't initially impressed by this while the dumbs trucked Winston only stared at her during the dance. After four years of having no communication at all, she ran into him at a dinner party and this time, they started to like each other. After a few months of courtship, they got married in 1908.

Despite their differences, Clementine and Churchill had a mostly peaceful marriage. Due to Churchill's hectic schedule, they spend much of their time apart, yet he considered her his rock. Clementine was never involved with the government but helped mold one of the greatest statesmen in history. She stood by his side throughout his journey, counseling him on complex political issues and diplomatic relations, even when he risked nearly everything to become a prime minister. She never hesitated to share her opinion especially when she told off Charles de Gaulle, the man behind the Free French forces in resisting capitulation to Germany throughout World War II who have become provisional president of France withinside the on the spot aftermath of the war, for insinuating that the French would turn their guns to the British instead of helping them defeat the Nazis. She also boosted his confidence during his grueling bouts with depression. In 1943, her husband had pneumonia and heart problems. She flew right away to Carthage to be by his side and to nurse him back to health. She provided the strength he needed to bounce back and lead a country in crisis. In their 57-year-long marriage, Clementine would constantly whisk him out of danger. However, their domestic life also became the stuff of urban legends. One incident claimed that Clementine once hurled a plate of spinach at Churchill during an argument over money. It was also said that when she could not take the stress, she would suffer from at least one breakdown and would leave for a vacation alone. In 1935, she allegedly had an affair with the artist, Terence Philip.

The Churchill family was not as perfect as they seemed to be. They were blessed with five children: Diana, Randolph, Sarah, Marigold, and Mary. Clementine spent little time with them as her efforts were poured into supporting her husband's political career. However, when the two-year-old Marigold died, the couple was severely devastated that they decided to raise Mary differently. She was their only child who grew up without grappling with alcohol addiction, marital problems, or suicidal tendencies. Diana, their eldest daughter, killed herself through overdosing on drugs in the 1960s, while Randolph also attempted to take his life several times. On the other hand, Sarah married three times—once without her parents' knowledge.

Fireside Question 16

†††

Clementine Hozier Churchill and Winston Churchill's story began in 1904. They eventually got married in four years after a short courtship despite their wide age gap. Do you think this became a factor in their relationship that lasted 57 years? Explain.

_____

_____

_____

_____

_____

_____

_____

_____

_____

_____

Fireside Question 17

†††

Clementine Hozier Churchill was born and raised by aristocratic parents and a product of a family marred rumor and scandal. How did this influence Clementine's relationship with Churchill and her parenting style? Did this have something to do with how she took great care of Churchill's reputation as a statesman?

_____

_____

_____

_____

_____

_____

_____

_____

_____

Fireside Question 18

†††

Despite their differences, they mostly had a peaceful marriage. Churchill considered Clementine, who stood by him until the end of their marriage, as his rock. What was Clementine's role in Churchill's political career? Cite some instances where she provided him support.

_____

_____

_____

_____

_____

_____

_____

_____

_____

_____

Fireside Question 19

†††

Clementine was the driving force behind Winston Churchill's success and fame. What are your goals? Who or what inspires you as you pursue your goals?

_____

_____

_____

_____

_____

_____

_____

_____

_____

_____

Fireside Question 20

†††

Clementine's children grew up without enough supervision. Amongst them, it was only Mary who was properly taken care of. What was Celemtine's parenting style? How did this adversely affect her children?

_____

_____

_____

_____

_____

_____

_____

_____

_____

_____

_____

Chapter Five: Inspiration and Influence behind Person and Work

†††

In a time of great despair and difficulty, only a few are willing to stand up and lead the populace. Amidst the crises of the twentieth century, several men and women took the challenge of governing the public. However, it could be argued that one man rose higher than many others and helped reunite a divided world, distinguishing himself as one of the greatest leaders of all time. This incredible man is none other than the former Prime Minister of Great Britain, Sir Winston Leonard Spencer-Churchill, who's a descendant of the Duke of Marlborough's aristocratic family. Though coming from a family of great privilege, Churchill's potential wouldn't be harnessed and developed without the guidance, influence and inspiration from these people:

His Parents, Lord Randolph Churchill (1849-1895) and Jennie Spencer-Churchill (1854-1921)

Sadly, from many accounts, it is known that Churchill grew in a distant and unaffectionate family environment. His father, Lord Randolph Churchill, was a conservative British statesman who was devoted to his political career to the detriment of his family. Shortly after Churchill's birth, his grandfather was made the Viceroy of Ireland and appointed his son as his secretary. On the other hand, his mother Jennie Spencer-Churchill, also known as Lady Randolph Churchill, was an American socialite. His absentee mother was a constant figure in Britain's social scene, so Churchill and his brother, Jack, were entrusted under the care of their nanny, Ms. Everest.

Despite his distant relationship with his parents, Churchill appeared to respect and love them deeply. He admired his father's skill and determination in politics and compared his mother's splendor to that of an evening star. Indeed, this apparent parental neglect only proved to strengthen Churchill, instilling within him a sense of determination to make his parents proud.

Elizabeth Ann Everest (1833-1895)

She was the nurse/nanny that raised Sir Winston Churchill. She had a natural and intuitive understanding of his physical and emotional needs during his formative years. As Churchill grew older and attended school, his pleas for his parents to regularly visit him went primarily ignored, and had it not been for Ms. Everest, he would have been very lonely. She became his personal confidant, as she always listened to him with sympathetic ears. It had been said that she was undoubtedly his "central emotional prop" during childhood.

Ms Everest also taught him many things and instilled within him an understanding of the life of a common Englishman. But what was deeply ingrained upon the young Winston through her was that serving others' needs was an arduous yet rewarding task. He realized that in helping others, one must listen, empathize, and gain the trust of the individuals being served. She may have abruptly left the Churchills, but her influence lasted within the future leader's heart.

Edward Gibbon (1737-1794)

Gibbon's The History of the Decline and Fall of the Roman Empire, known for the quality and irony of its prose, its use of primary sources, and slander of organized religion, greatly influenced Sir Winston Churchill's governmental and diplomatic strategies. Through the principles stated in the book, Churchill crafted his own opinions on legislative and administrative issues. Most of all he adopted its main ideology of fighting for what you believe is right.

Fireside Question 21

†††

Sir Winston Churchill was born in a prominent and wealthy English family but was deprived of love and affection from his absentee parents. Who instead nurtured and cared for the young Winston? What were her teachings that Churchill carried into adulthood?

_____

_____

_____

_____

_____

_____

_____

_____

_____

_____

Fireside Question 22

Churchill admired his father's skill and determination in politics and compared his mother's splendor to that of an evening star. What were the achievements of his parents in the political and social sphere? Do you think it bore tremendous pressure on the young Winston?

_____

_____

_____

_____

_____

_____

_____

_____

_____

_____

Fireside Question 23

††††

Though coming from a family of great privilege, Churchill's great potential wouldn't be harnessed and developed without the guidance, influence and inspiration from a number of people. Among all the people listed above, who do you think had the most impact and played the most vital role in his life? Why is that so?

Fireside Question 24

†††

Ms Everest also taught the young Winston many things and instilled within him an understanding of the life of a common Englishman.How would you describe the life of the commoners? Why is this knowledge important to a statesman like Churchill?

_____

_____

_____

_____

_____

_____

_____

_____

_____

_____

_____

Fireside Question 25

†††

Gibbon's The History of the Decline and Fall of the Roman Empire, known for the quality and irony of its prose, its use of primary sources, and slander of organized religion, greatly influenced Sir Winston Churchill's governmental and diplomatic strategies. What was the main principle of Gibbon's book? How did Churchill apply this in his career as a politician?

Chapter Six: Main Accomplishments and Notable Achievements

Did You Know?

Winston Churchill loved to smoke and drink. He would do anything so that his vices won't be compromised. Traveling by airplane was required during World War II, so he had his oxygen mask customized in a way that still allowed smoking. In addition to that, Churchill took 60 bottles of alcohol with him when he set out for the Boer War.

††††

Winston Churchill was known for his great achievements throughout his career. He was selected as a Member of Parliament from the constituency of Oldham even before his political career began and became a part of the Cabinet as President of the Board of Trade in 1908. During his term, he passed the Trade Boards Act of 1900, which established the first minimum wage system in Britain by mandating salary rates for 200,000 workers in several industries. The Mines Act of 1908 directed an 8-hour workday in all mines, and the Labour Exchanges Act of 1909 helped the jobless find employment.

He had an active participation in the passage of the People's Budget. —
Introduced in the British Parliament by David Lloyd George, Churchill
supported the budget, which proposed unprecedented taxes on the wealthy to
fund radical social welfare programs. It was considered as the first attempt in
British history to redistribute wealth among the public. During his early
political career, he also played an active role in bringing about radical social
reforms. These became known as Liberal Welfare Reforms, which included
providing pension to those over 70, giving children free school meals, and
allowing tenant farmers to tend to their land without their landlords'
interference.

He implemented naval reforms as the First Lord of the Admiralty. —
Sir Winston Churchill was promoted as the Home Secretary in 1910. His
term saw the implementation of the National Insurance Act of 1911, which
provided obligatory medical insurance coverage for workers who earn an
annual salary lower than £160. It is considered as one of the foundations of
present-day social government assistance in the UK. In 1911, Churchill was
appointed as the First Lord of the Admiralty, a post he held until 1915. His
essential contributions in this capacity were naval reforms, such as the
establishment of the Royal Naval Air Service, a department of maritime
aviation, in 1912; the adoption of more powerful firearms as the main
armament of British battleships; and the modernization of coal-powered
vessels into the faster and more high-powered oil-powered warships.
Churchill additionally supported the development of the tank as a combat
weapon during World War II, which was financed from the naval exploration
reserves.

He was the War and Air Secretary as well as the Colonial Secretary in the early 1920s. — Sir Winston Churchill served as the Secretary of State for War and the Secretary of State for Air from 1919 to 1921. He was responsible for demobilizing the rebels in the British Somaliland after the First World War, effectively bringing an end to their 20-year resistance; and for crushing the Iraqi revolt against the British in 1920. He was then appointed as Secretary of State for the Colonies in 1921 to 1922.where he negotiated the Anglo-Irish Treaty of 1921.It established the Irish Free State and protected the British maritime interests by allowing the Royal Navy access to three Irish ports.

Winston Churchill was appointed as Prime Minister of the UK during the Second World War. — After five years of a horrible term as the Chancellor of the Exchequer, Churchill remained politically powerless for the more significant part of the 1930s. During this time, he passionately cautioned against Germany's rearmament, called on Britain to strengthen itself to counter German belligerence, and fiercely criticized Prime Minister Neville Chamberlain's appeasement of German Chancellor Adolf Hitler. U.K. eventually declared war on Germany, following the outbreak of World War II on the 3rd of September 1939 and he was reappointed as the First Lord of the Admiralty. During the Battle of France, Chamberlain abandoned his position and Churchill subsequently became the Prime Minister of the United Kingdom on the 10th of May 1940. He remained in office until the 26th of July 1945, successfully leading Great Britain through the Second World War.

He united and inspired Britain with his proficient leadership during World War II. — Upon becoming Prime Minister, Churchill formed a coalition cabinet of leaders from the Labour, Liberal and Conservative parties. He made sure it represented all groups and was able to make swift decisions. Though he dominated the Parliament, he ensured that it was free from domestic and political conflicts. He rejected Germany's talks of surrender and proposal for a peace treaty. Instead, he gave his electrifying "This was their finest hour" speech wherein he asked the populace to prepare for the Battle of Britain, urging them to "brace [themselves]to [their] duties.". He delivered stirring speeches in the Parliament and on the radio to unite the nation against Germany. Under his leadership, Britain handed the Germans their first significant defeat in the Battle of Britain in 1940.

Together with Franklin Roosevelt and Joseph Stalin, Winston Churchill led the Allied Coalition to victory during World War II. — Churchill had an excellent relationship with United States President Franklin D. Roosevelt with whom he held several conferences to cover various war policies. When Adolf Hitler launched his attack on the Soviet Union, Churchill unequivocally vowed to support Stalindespite his vehement anti-communist views. Subsequently, the United States entered World War II following the attack on Pearl Harbor. Churchill worked closely with the two leaders to form the grand alliance among the three nations. Churchill, Roosevelt and Stalin, known as the 'Big Three' of the Allied Coalition, were instrumental in implementing a war strategy that resulted in the defeat of Axis Powers in the Second World War.

From 1951 to 1955, Sir Winston Churchill served as the British Prime Minister for a second term. — Despite effectively leading Britain in World War II, Churchill lost the 1945 general election. Instead, he became the

Leader of the Opposition for six years. He was reelected Prime Minister during the general election of October 1951 and served until his resignation in April 1955. Domestic reforms enacted in his subsequent term include, the Mines and Quarries Act of 1954, which standardized the work hours of miners and ensured their security, health and wellbeing and the Housing Repairs and Rent Act of 1955, which expanded past housing acts to define the standards of housing fit for human habitation. Internationally his second tenure saw rebellions in Kenya and Malaya, to which he controversially responded with direct military action.

Sir Winston Churchill won the 1953 Nobel Prize in Literature. — As a prominent prolific writer, his oeuvre includes a novel, two biographies, three volumes of memoirs, and several historical accounts. During his early career, he wrote for The Pioneer, The Daily Telegraph and The Morning Post. In 1898, his first work, The Story of the Malakand Field Force, was published. His famous works include a four-volume history of Britain and its colonies, A History of the English-Speaking Peoples (1956–1958), and The Second World War (1948–1953), a book series in six volumes. which was a major critical and commercial success. He earned the Nobel Prize in Literature in 1953 for his extensive and significant body of work. Apart from being an acclaimed nonfiction writer, Churchill had a brief career in the British Army where he fought as Lieutenant during the Battle of Omdurman in 1898. He was also an artist whose best-known paintings were Impressionist landscapes.

The Greatest Briton in history. — In 1941, he was selected as a Fellow of the Royal Society. In 1953, he became a member of the Noblest Order of the Garter, the highest order of chivalry in the U.K. In 1963, he became the first of only eight people to be made an honorary citizen of the United States. He was also included in the 20th century's 100 Most Influential People List and was also hailed as one of the most influential leaders in history by TIME. In 2002, the BBC conducted a television poll to determine the 100 Greatest Britons in history. Based on approximately a million votes, Churchill was voted "The Greatest of Them All."

Fireside Question 26

†††

Sir Winston Churchill flourished in his chosen fields. The text mentions several of his accomplishments. What do you think is Sir Winston Churchill's most significant accomplishment? Why is that so?

_____

_____

_____

_____

_____

_____

_____

_____

_____

_____

_____

Fireside Question 27

†††

Despite his extreme anti-communist views, Sir Winston Churchill unequivocally vowed to support the Soviet Union. Do you think having a change of heart and different points of view benefited him? In what way?

_____

_____

_____

_____

_____

_____

_____

_____

_____

_____

Fireside Question 28

†††

Sir Winston Churchill excelled and thrived in his career both as a statesman and as a writer. Who do you think played a substantial role in his achievements? Why?

_____

_____

_____

_____

_____

_____

_____

_____

_____

_____

Fireside Question 29

††ized†

He served as the British Prime Minister for a second term. What do you think is the most essential reform he implemented? Why is that so?

_____

_____

_____

_____

_____

_____

_____

_____

_____

_____

Fireside Question 30

†††

Sir Winston Churchill's achievements are listed in school textbooks and are taught in schools nowadays. What is his lasting legacy? Do you think it still has an impact in today's society? Discuss.

_____

_____

_____

_____

_____

_____

_____

_____

_____

_____

_____

Attention: Get Your Free Gift Now

Every <u>purchase</u> now comes with a FREE Bonus Gift

2020 Top 5 Fireside Books of the Year

(New-York Times Bestsellers, USA Today & more)

<u>Get it now here:</u>

<u>Scan QR Code to Download Free Gift</u>

q ``

Printed in Great Britain
by Amazon